ECO STEAM

the
STUFF
WE BUY

GEORGIA AMSON-BRADSHAW

WAYLAND

Published in paperback in Great Britain in 2020 by Wayland

 Produced for Wayland by
White-Thomson Publishing Ltd
www.wtpub.co.uk

Series Editor: Georgia Amson-Bradshaw
Series Designer: Rocket Design (East Anglia) Ltd

ISBN: 978 1 5263 0793 4
10 9 8 7 6 5 4 3 2 1

Wayland
An imprint of
Hachette Children's Group
Part of Hodder & Stoughton
Carmelite House
50 Victoria Embankment
London EC4Y 0DZ

An Hachette UK Company
www.hachette.co.uk
www.hachettechildrens.co.uk

Printed in Dubai

!

**Adult
supervision is
recommended when
using the internet**

Picture acknowledgements:
4t bondgrunge, 4b tele52, 5t Artisticco, 5c Anna Frajtova, 5b RTimages, 6l StockSmartStart, 6r petovarga,
7t Pix One, 7c Rich Carey, 7b lenina11only, 8c Climber 1959, 8t Zhenyakot, 8b Rocket, 9t Aun Photographer,
9c Michele Paccione, 9b LuckyVector, 10t Han Aji, 10c Chinchilla16, 10b GoodStudio, 11t matrioshka,
11c Julio Yeste, 11b Dmitry Kalinovsky, 12t gomolach, 12bl mei yanotai, 12br Samot, 13t sirtravelalot,
13c Aleutie, 14t Andrew Rybalko, 15b Audiowawe, 16t Viktoria Kazakova, 16c FashionStock.com. 16b Elopaint,
17b CRS PHOTO, 18c Natalia Kuzmina, 18b Dmitry Yakolev, 19b los_ojos_pardos, 20c Andrix Tkacenko, 20br
Tatiana Gulyaeva, 20bl Strike Pattern, 21t Pretty Vector, 24t People Image Studio, 24c Rocket, 24b Rich Carey,
25t Dawena Moore, 25c naulicreative, 25b Andrew Rybalko, 26t Li Chaoshu, 26b Li Chaoshu, 27t simonkr,
27c Rocket, 27b Ekaterina Pankina, 28cl Man As Thep, 28cr brown32, 28b Golden Sikorka, 29tr Abscent, 32t
gst, 32c Mikadun, 32b petovarga, 33c Peter Essick, 33b Rvector, 34t Golden Sikorka, 34b Vlad Teodor, 35t
matrioshka, 35c kao, 35b petovarga, 36t petovarga, 36cl macrovector, 36cr gaynor, 37bl Rvector,
38t macrovector, 37cr petovarga, 37cl BSVIT, 40t gradyreese, 40b patineegvector, 41cr Rocket, 41b ImYanis,
42t ProStcokStudio. 42c Graf Vishenka, 42b Sky Pics Studio, 43b Sabelskaya, 44 Rocket, 45 petovarga, 45
macrovector, 45 gaynor, 45 Rvector, 45 macrovector, 45 petovarga, 45 BSVIT, 46t Ilya Bolotov, 46c Gabriel12,
46b sirtravelalot

Illustrations on pages 30, 31 and 39 by Steve Evans.

All design elements from Shutterstock.

CONTENTS

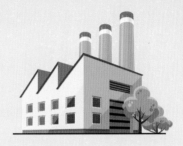

MATERIAL WORLD

Look around you. Unless you're reading this book naked in the middle of a forest, you'll be surrounded by stuff that humans have made. That stuff is made from materials that have been extracted or harvested, processed and probably transported great distances before they reached you.

Raw materials

The things we own are made from all sorts of raw materials. What do you have that's made of plastic? Plastic is made from crude oil extracted from deep underground. How about something metal? Metal comes from ores which are found in rocks. Rubber, cotton and paper are made from different types of plants. Some of the resources we rely on are renewable (meaning we can keep making more of them), but some of the most widely used materials are not.

Metal ore is mined from the ground.

Demand for materials

Since 1970, the demand for natural resources has more than tripled, as more and more things are made and sold around the world. But although the trade in goods keeps increasing, the natural world which provides the raw materials isn't getting any bigger. Even renewable materials from plants need land to grow on, which we can't make more of. This growing demand is not sustainable – meaning it cannot be carried on indefinitely.

The number of containers of goods shipped by sea is predicted to quadruple by 2030.

Consumption

The demand for materials is driven by consumption, which means buying and using stuff. Some of the things we buy, such as toothbrushes or underpants, are essentials. But other things, such as that brand new TV to replace the perfectly working – but slightly smaller – old one, are not essential.

SPOTLIGHT: CONSUMERISM

When you buy and use something, you are being a consumer. Consumerism is driven by the idea that it's good to keep amassing new things.

Why buy?

There are lots of reasons why people keep buying new things. Sometimes they need to replace an item that has broken. But a lot of the time, people buy new things not because they need them, but because they want them. Perhaps they don't want to be the only person without a particular new piece of clothing or the latest smartphone. Having new things makes people feel good.

We are surrounded by advertisements that try to make us want new things.

NEW FOR SPRING

MAKING THINGS, MAKING WASTE

What happens to your stuff when you don't want it anymore? It often goes straight into the bin, and sent to landfill, meaning it gets dumped in a hole in the ground. At best, it gets recycled, but even our current recycling systems can't make use of 100 per cent of what we throw away because many things aren't made to be recyclable in the first place.

91% of plastic waste is not recycled.

Linear system

At the moment, the way we make, use and dispose of stuff is a 'linear system'. That means that it follows a line of steps:

1 **Extraction**, where raw materials such as wood and ores are harvested or taken out of the ground.

2 **Production**, where the raw materials are made into products to be sold and used.

3 **Distribution**, where those products are transported to shops around the world.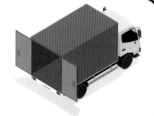

4 **Consumption**, where the products are bought by customers and used.

5 **Disposal**, where the products are thrown away.

System problems

The linear system depends on two basic ideas: firstly, that there will always be raw materials that can be extracted, and secondly, that there will always be an "away" to throw our unwanted things to. But it's becoming clear that this is not going to be the case.

Oil is used to make fuels, plastic and various chemicals, including medicines. But it is a non-renewable resource, so in a linear system it will eventually run out.

Disposable world

Over the last few decades, there has been a large increase in the amount of single-use, disposable products being made and sold, such as plastic drinks bottles, food packaging, coffee cups and more. Because so little of this plastic is recycled, it becomes pollution. More than eight million tonnes of tonnes of plastic waste end up in the oceans each year (right).

Too much waste

It isn't just the things that consumers buy and throw away that become waste. Even if we recycled everything we bought, waste would still be created during the extraction and production stages. This is because usable resources, such as metal, need to be separated from the rest of the raw material, such as the rocks they come from.

A pile of waste from metal extraction

THE ISSUE:
TOO MUCH STUFF

Most people who live in well-off countries have a lot of stuff. The average American home contains around 300,000 separate items, and even though average house size has nearly tripled in the USA in the last 50 years, more and more people are renting private storage space in which to put their extra things. Making all these things has a big environmental impact.

The average British 10-year-old has 238 toys, but plays with only 12 of them.

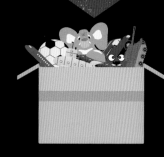

Energy use

Processing materials such as plastic, wood and metal into finished products uses huge amounts of energy. Most of this energy is generated by burning fossil fuels, which releases gases such as carbon dioxide. Referred to as greenhouse gases, they stay in the Earth's atmosphere, trapping heat from the Sun and causing climate change, which disrupts natural weather patterns around the world.

This factory produces chipboard from wood.

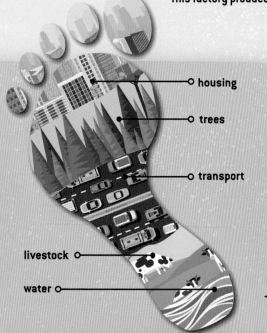

- housing
- trees
- transport
- livestock
- water

SPOTLIGHT: ECOLOGICAL FOOTPRINT

Your ecological footprint describes the amount of resources that are needed to support the life you live. The resources include things like land and water, and take into account factors such as how much pollution and greenhouse gases your lifestyle creates.

Transporting stuff

Energy and materials are needed not only to make things, but to transport them too. Around 90 per cent of the world's goods are transported by sea in large cargo ships. Cargo ships run on fossil fuels and release greenhouse gases. These ships alone release over 2 per cent of the entire world's greenhouse gas emissions.

Three and a half billion tons of cargo passes through Europe's 1,200 seaports each year.

richest

poorest

Resource-use gap

Many people in well-off countries live a consumption-heavy lifestyle; this is very different to how many other people live around the world. The world's richest countries consume on average 10 times as many materials as the poorest. This means two things: we are consuming the world's resources in an unsustainable way and the use of these resources is not evenly shared.

If everyone in the world lived like the average Australian, we'd need five planet Earths.

If everyone lived like the average Vietnamese person, we could live on an Earth 10 per cent smaller.

HOW THINGS ARE PRODUCED

Today's high levels of consumption wouldn't be possible without the technology that allows goods to be produced very quickly and very cheaply. Most of our gadgets and toys, the furniture and appliances in our homes and the clothes we wear are mass-produced. This is very different to how things were made in the past.

Made by hand

For most of history, objects, clothing, vehicles — anything that was man-made — were produced one at a time either at home or by craftspeople. A shirt would be stitched by hand either in the home or by a tailor. A wagon would be built using hand tools by a carpenter.

Made to order

Because making things by hand is very time-consuming, even simple objects would have been very expensive compared to today. Shops crammed full of goods waiting for people to buy them did not exist in the same way — instead craftspeople sat in workshops waiting to take orders.

Hand tools in a recreation of a medieval carpenter's workshop

In Tudor times, a plain shirt worn by a servant would have cost up to £800 in modern money. This is because every step, from making the material to the finished garment, was done by hand.

DIVISION OF LABOUR

During the process of making an object, separate tasks can be assigned to different people. For example, in making a shoe, one person might make the sole, while another stitches the upper part. This is called 'division of labour'. It can be applied on a small scale, but is a key technique used in mass production.

Assembly line

A key moment in the development of mass production was the advent of Henry Ford's Model T car. This was the first time that cars were built on an assembly line, where each worker remains in place with a specific task to do. The car itself moves along the line, being built step by step. This technique is very fast, and a Model T was soon being produced every ten seconds.

A Ford Model T car

Modern production

Nowadays, many consumer goods are produced in a similar way. A lot of the work in factories mass-producing goods is done by people in less well-off countries where the pay is low. These methods allow goods to be sold very cheaply, encouraging people to buy more and more stuff.

A worker putting computer mice together on an assembly line in China.

SOLVE IT!
REDUCE OVERCONSUMPTION

The increasing trend of people buying ever more stuff, and using more and more raw materials is not sustainable. But many of the things we buy are fun or useful. Can you see how we could still get use out of things we need, while helping to reduce overconsumption?

FACT ONE →

In the year 2000, 2,441 million CDs were sold around the world. In 2015, 569 million physical CDs were sold. The number declined as people streamed music online instead.

FACT TWO

Many cities around the world have put in place public bicycle hire schemes where people can pick up a bike on the street and pay a small amount of money to use it.

FACT THREE

New companies have started up in several countries that offer clothes on a subscription basis. People pay a monthly fee to have fashionable clothes delivered to them each month, which they return after wearing them for a few weeks.

FACT FOUR →

'Swishing' is an activity that has become popular, where groups of people come together, each bringing a few items of clothing, books or furniture, which they then swap. Everyone comes away with 'new' items.

FACT FIVE

Freecycle is an online platform that was launched in 2003. On it, people post notices of goods that they don't want anymore, offering them to other local people for free, instead of throwing them away.

 CAN YOU SOLVE IT?

Look at all of the examples given here. How are each of these examples enabling people to get new things without contributing to the problems of overconsumption?

► What is the one key fact that they all have in common?

► How do they achieve the same kind of outcome in different ways?

Feeling confused? Answer on page 42.

TEST IT!
BUILD A SWAP SHOP SITE

Don't throw out clothes that don't fit you anymore or games you've finished playing. Swap them with people you know instead by creating your own swap shop website. Ask an adult before using the internet.

YOU WILL NEED

a computer with internet access

STEP ①

Go online to find a website builder (also called a content management system). These are websites such as Wix, Weebly or Squarespace that let you build your own website online. Check out how much they cost before you start, as some charge a monthly fee or charge for some features. Wix has no monthly fee or costs for adding forums to your site.

STEP ②

Sign up with your email address. The first step is to choose a theme for your site. This is the basic style and layout for your website, but don't worry about choosing a perfect one as they can all be completely customised.

STEP ③

Add a forum to your site. These are usually referred to as 'apps' on the website builder, so look in the app menu to add a forum page.

STEP ④

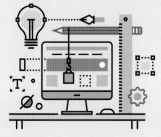

Play with the design and content of your website, changing colours, pictures, text or getting rid of features on the template that you don't want. All website builders work slightly differently, so try clicking around the menus and the buttons to see what you can do. You can also use the Help function to find out how to make changes. Keep playing around until you like the look.

TIP

If you want, you can password-protect your site, so only people who have the password can access it. Search the Help section for 'password protect' to see how to do this.

STEP ⑤

Edit the forum page on your website so it has a section for 'Offers' and a section for 'Wanted'. These are the places where people can post things they don't want any more, or things they would like to have.

STEP ⑥

When your site is ready, click 'publish' and it will go live online. Give the password to your friends or people at school. Get them to sign up and get swapping!

your site name

forum for things offered

the swap shop   Login / Sign up

WELCOME TO
THE SWAP SHOP

OFFERS
Put things you don't want anymore here.

2 Posts

WANTED
Put things you want here.

4 Posts

forum for things wanted

THE ISSUE:
THROWAWAY FASHION

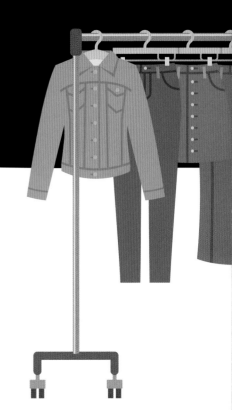

Our clothes keep us warm, and are an important part of how we express our personalities. For many people, wearing clothes that are in fashion and follow the latest trends makes them feel good. But our clothes are being worn for less and less time before being thrown away, and very little clothing is recycled.

Disposable clothes

In the last 15 years, the amount of clothing being made each year has doubled, largely due to 'fast fashion', where people buy cheap versions of the latest trends then throw them away. Around half of these clothes are chucked out after less than a year, and some garments may be worn fewer than ten times before being disposed of.

High street stores sell cheap versions of runway fashions that are mass-produced for retail.

Not recycled

Globally, a tiny one per cent of the materials used in clothing is recycled to make new clothing, and only 12 per cent is recycled for other uses such as making felt or insulation materials. The majority of textiles (meaning cloth, or fabric) are sent to landfill or are burned.

ONE EVERY SECOND

Every single second, the equivalent of one garbage truck of textiles is sent to landfill or burned.

Plastic pollution

The world's most popular fibre (see page 18) for making textiles with is polyester, which is a type of plastic. It is cheap to produce and can be made into many different forms, making it ideal for fast fashion. But when we wash plastic textiles in the washing machine, tiny bits called microfibres get washed off. These are too small to be filtered out in water treatment plants, so they end up in the ocean where they contribute to plastic pollution.

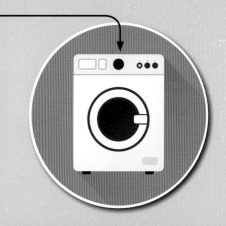

Cotton impacts

The second most popular fibre in the world is cotton. Unlike plastic fabrics, cotton comes from a plant, making it a renewable material. However, most cotton production still has serious effects on the environment. Just 2.4 per cent of the world's farmland is used to grow cotton, but cotton farming accounts for 24 per cent of global pesticide use. Pesticides have a big impact on surrounding ecosystems, as well as harming workers' health. Cotton also requires vast amounts of water to grow, and in many cotton-growing areas local supplies of fresh water are being drained to irrigate the crops.

An irrigation system waters a field of cotton plants in Maharashtra, India.

PRODUCING TEXTILES

Textiles are made from fibres, which are thin threads of natural or synthetic (man-made) material. Most natural fibres, such as cotton or linen, are short. These are twisted together to make a long strand of yarn. Synthetic fibres, such as polyester, are long. They are made by stretching out molten plastic into fine strands.

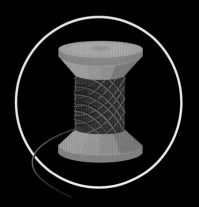

A cotton boll

Natural fibres

There are many types of natural fibres from animal and plant sources. Cotton grows on plants, in a fluffy 'boll' that is like cotton wool. Linen and hemp fibres grow inside the stalks of plants. Wool comes from various animals, including sheep and alpaca.

Semi-synthetic fibres

Some fibres, such as lyocell or viscose, are called 'semi-synthetic'. This is because the raw material is natural – lyocell and viscose are made from wood, bamboo or soya plants. But unlike cotton or linen, the fibres are artificially created. The wood or bamboo is dissolved into a pulp using chemicals, then squeezed out through tiny holes to form strands, in a similar way to how fully artificial fibres such as polyester are made.

Lyocell is made from the pulp of eucalyptus trees.

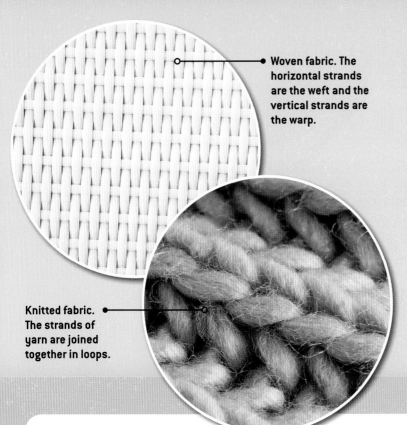

Woven fabric. The horizontal strands are the weft and the vertical strands are the warp.

Knitted fabric. The strands of yarn are joined together in loops.

Making fabric

Strands of yarn are woven or knitted together to make sheets of fabric. In woven fabric, horizontal strands of yarn are criss-crossed with vertical strands of yarn. Knitted fabrics are made by looping strands of yarn together. The way that you weave or knit the yarn together has an effect on the texture and appearance of the finished fabric.

SPOTLIGHT: ORGANIC TEXTILES

Organic fibres are grown without the use of chemical fertilisers or potentially toxic pesticides, and any chemicals used during production meet strict requirements on how toxic they are, and whether they biodegrade. Making textiles from organic fibres is more environmentally friendly.

Qualities of fabric

Depending on the fibres used, and the way that the yarn has been woven or knitted together, the finished fabric will have different qualities. Woven cotton, for example, is cool to wear, soft and creases easily. Knitted woollen fabric is warm, can be soft or coarse and creases drop out quickly. Choosing the best fabric for a particular garment will depend on what qualities are needed. There isn't much point in making a summer shirt out of heavy, knitted wool!

Wool is well suited to making warm winter clothing.

SOLVE IT!
SUSTAINABLE CLOTHING

The way we currently buy and dispose of clothing is having an increasingly serious impact on the environment. We can change the way we shop for and get rid of clothing to help reduce that impact. Using the information below, can you figure out what we should be doing differently?

FACT ONE

Most cotton is grown using a lot of pesticides and other chemicals, but organic cotton is also available.

100%
ORGANIC

FACT TWO

Hemp is a plant that can be turned into fabric. It requires less water to grow than cotton, and can easily be grown without pesticides and other chemicals.

FACT THREE

Artificial fibres such as polyester are washed off clothes during laundry cycles. This results in billions of plastic microfibres polluting our oceans.

FACT FOUR

Extending the average use of clothes saves water and energy, but very few people repair clothes nowadays, throwing away damaged garments instead.

FACT FIVE

As long as the textiles are usable, old clothes can be upcycled (made into something new without destroying the original object) or recycled (broken down back into materials and reformed into new things).

FACT SIX

Textiles that are 100 per cent natural, such as cotton, can be composted when they cannot be recycled any more.

CAN YOU SOLVE IT?

Now you know these facts about clothing and textiles, how would you advise people on ways to reduce the impact their clothing choices have on the environment? Design a simple poster to inform people with the headings **CHOOSE, USE, LOSE**. On it, explain:

► What type of clothing or textiles should people CHOOSE when they are shopping?

► How should people USE their clothing differently?

► What is the best way to LOSE or dispose of old clothing?

Not quite sure? Turn to page 43 for ideas.

TEST IT!
UPCYCLED T-SHIRT

Do you have an old T-shirt that you love, but that no longer fits? Don't chuck it out! Upcycle it into a drawstring gym bag with this no-sew upcycling project instead.

YOU WILL NEED

an old T-shirt

a roll of cord or strong ribbon

two large safety pins

scissors

STEP ①

Turn the T-shirt inside out and lay it on a flat surface. Cut the ends off the sleeves, so that the sleeves end in a vertical edge, rather than an angled edge.

STEP ②

Every two centimetres, make cuts in the sleeves that reach the seam, creating short 'tags' of fabric. As well as on the sleeves, make 4-cm deep cuts every couple of cm around the bottom hem of the T-shirt, too.

STEP ③

Tie each of the opposite pairs of tags together along the sleeves and the hem of the T-shirt. By tying opposite tags together, you are sealing up the holes where the sleeves were and along the bottom of the shirt.

STEP ④

Flip the T-shirt the right way out, so the tied tags are on the inside. Make two very small snips in the hem on either side of the T-shirt neck. Don't cut through the seam.

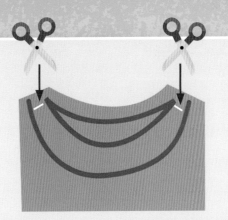

STEP ⑤

Cut two lengths of cord. Each piece of cord should be about four times as long as the T-shirt is tall. Attach a safety pin to one end of the first piece of cord, and push it into the snip you made in one side of the neck hem. Wriggle the safety pin and attached cord all the way around the neck and back out the same hole. Pull it so that the two ends are of equal length.

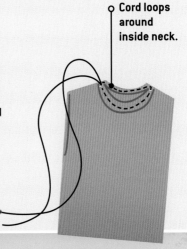

Cord loops around inside neck.

STEP ⑥

Repeat the last step with the other piece of cord, but entering and exiting the hole on the opposite side of the neck. This creates your drawstring in the top of the bag, and the bag's straps.

Second cord loops opposite way.

STEP ⑦

Tie knots at the end of the cord straps. Safety pin the ends of the straps through the knots to the bottom two corners of the bag. Trim any excess cord. Your bag is complete!

THE ISSUE:

PROBLEMS WITH PAPER

Paper is amazing stuff – it has enabled people around the world to learn to read and write, and is a crucial material for communication. But we use an awful lot of paper, and there are problems with the way it is currently produced and used, which are adding to the pressures on precious natural forests and wildlife.

The average German person uses 6.35 trees per year in paper. The average Indian person uses 0.23.

Deforestation

Paper is made from wood from trees, which are a renewable resource. However, not every tree can be easily replaced. Rainforests contain delicate and important ecosystems, with many types of slow-growing trees that provide habitats for a range of other living things. In some countries, rainforests are being cut down and replaced with fast-growing tree plantations that don't support the same ecosystems.

A paper mill in Florida, USA. The US paper industry released about 79,000 tonnes of air and water pollution in 2015.

Resource-use and pollution

Turning the raw material wood into the finished product of paper uses a lot of resources. It takes energy to harvest the wood and run the paper-making machines. Very large quantities of water are used throughout paper-making, as the fibres from the wood are mixed with a lot of water to make pulp (read about this on the next page). If the paper is bleached or dyed, this also uses a lot of chemicals which sometimes get released into waterways, causing pollution.

Recycled paper creates 35% less water pollution and 74% less air pollution than paper from new wood.

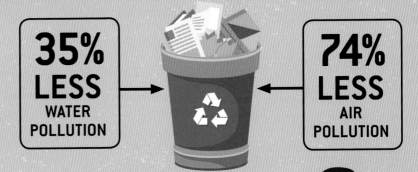

35% LESS WATER POLLUTION

74% LESS AIR POLLUTION

Wasteful printing

Because paper is a cheap material, it is often used in an unnecessarily wasteful way. A study showed that 45 per cent of the paper printed in offices is thrown away by the end of the day. A trillion sheets of paper per year have a lifespan of less than one day around the world. Unwanted junk mail is another big waste of paper. In the USA, an estimated 90 billion items of junk mail are sent annually. If they were stacked in a single pile it would reach halfway to the moon!

HOW PAPER IS MADE

Just like fabric, paper is made from fibres. Instead of being woven or knitted together, the fibres are pressed down and stuck together. If you tear a piece of paper or card and look very closely at it, you'll see it has a soft, almost fluffy edge where the fibres stick out.

Making pulp

The first stage of paper-making is making pulp. This can be done by machine, or using chemicals. The mechanical process chops and blends wood with water into a soup-like mixture. The chemical method boils the wood up with strong chemicals that dissolve it into the pulp. Dyes and other chemicals are then added to the pulp to change the appearance or texture of the finished paper.

A vat of paper pulp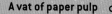

Rolling the paper

To turn the pulp into paper, it is processed through another machine. The pulp is first spread over a conveyor belt made of wire mesh. A lot of the water is removed at this stage by shaking and blowing the mesh with air. The pulp is now a damp mat of fibres, which is then pressed through a series of rollers. This squeezes the rest of the water out and makes large, flat sheets of paper which are stored on spools.

Paper being rolled onto a spool

Recycled paper

To recycle paper, it is separated into grades and types at a recycling plant. It is then washed with soapy water to remove inks, and other unwanted materials such as plastic film, staples and glue. The paper is mixed and mashed with water again to create pulp. The pulp is then rolled into new paper again.

Workers sorting paper at a recycling plant

Paper can only be recycled about five times before the fibres become too small to mat together into new paper.

Using other materials

Most paper is made from wood because trees have the highest amount of fibres per square hectare grown, but it can be made from all sorts of plant material. Small manufacturers around the world use all sorts of different resources, including farm waste such as cornstalks and soy-bean vines, discarded orange peel from juice factories and even animal dung!

All sorts of natural fibres can be used to make paper. You can make handmade paper from grass clippings!

SOLVE IT!
ECO-FRIENDLY PAPER

We can make improvements to global paper manufacturing at each stage of production, from growing the raw material and processing it, to use and disposal. Read the following pieces of information. What should we do to ensure our paper is less damaging to the environment?

FACT ONE

Most paper is made from trees. Some of these come from well-managed forests, but others come from plantations that have replaced rainforests.

FACT TWO

Paper can be made from other plant materials, such as waste stalks from farming.

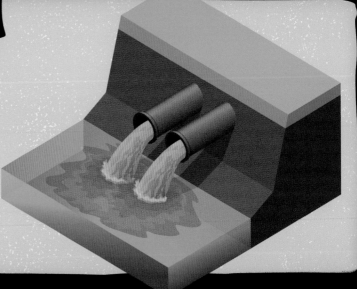

FACT THREE

Paper-making uses a lot of water. This is often simply pumped out into local waterways, but could be cleaned and reused.

FACT FOUR

Paper can be recycled. However, it can only be recycled a few times and the process uses energy and water. Reusing and using less paper helps save energy and water.

FACT FIVE

When unwanted paper is sent to landfill, it creates methane, a powerful greenhouse gas. However, because it is made of plant fibres, it can be composted.

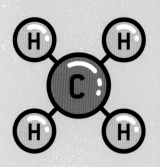

 # CAN YOU SOLVE IT?

Look at the facts listed here, and think about what else you know about how paper is made. Using this information, draw a flow chart that shows how we can produce, use and dispose of paper in a more eco-friendly way. On your flow chart:

▶ Draw pictures for each stage.

▶ Add labels with notes, for example explaining how people should (or shouldn't) use paper.

▶ Link the pictures with arrows.

Need some help? Turn to page 44 for an example.

TEST IT!
HANDMADE PAPER

Try making your own handmade recycled paper. It's a fun way to use old scrap paper, and is great for craft projects or handmade greetings cards.

YOU WILL NEED

a large bowl

scrap paper (roughly five sheets)

warm water

a blender

scissors

a wooden picture frame (without glass in it)

fine nylon fly screen material (available from hardware or garden stores)

a stapler

a large tub (larger than your picture frame)

several tea towels

an iron

STEP ①

Tear up the scrap paper into small pieces, a couple of centimetres across. Soak the torn scraps in a large bowl of warm water for about an hour.

STEP ②

While the paper is soaking, make the mould. Cut a square of fly screen that is the size of your picture frame. Staple the fly screen material to the picture frame around the edges.

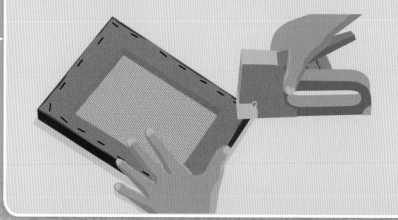

STEP ③

Put the soaked paper and water in the blender (ask an adult for help with this step). Mix it at half-speed until it is a smooth mix.

STEP ④

Fill the tub with water to a few centimetres deep. Pour the blended mixture into the water, and stir it to create the pulp. The pulp should be the texture of soup.

STEP ⑤

Dip your mould into the tub and swish it around to get an even layer of pulp on the screen. Rest it on the edge of the tub to let some water drip out. After a few minutes use a tea towel to gently blot more water away.

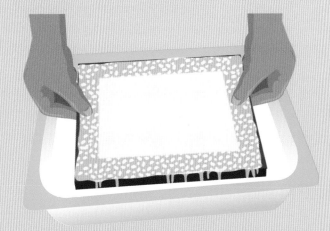

STEP ⑥

Place the frame pulp-side-down on another dry tea towel. Gently lift the screen. If the pulp doesn't come off, peel it away from the screen at the edge. If it is too wet to come away, leave it to dry for longer on a dry tea towel.

STEP ⑦

Cover the paper with another tea towel, then ask an adult to help you iron it. This will flatten it further. Leave your ironed sheets of paper to fully dry for a day or two. When totally dry, your paper is ready to use!

WASTE ELECTRONICS

How many electronic items does your family own, such as mobile phones, tablets, laptops, TVs, games consoles, digital cameras and so on? How old are each of those items? Many of us replace our electronic goods such as our mobile phones every year, and this consumption is creating a lot of waste.

Precious metals

An average smartphone may contain up to 62 different types of metal, including gold, copper and rare-earth metals which are extremely difficult to get out of the ground. These metals are mined in different countries around the world, and mining and processing them is a very dirty practice. Processing one tonne of rare-earth metals produces around 2,000 tonnes of toxic waste, and their ores often contain radioactive material.

Toxic chemicals from mining metals are released into waterways, such as this pollution from a copper mine in Romania.

Unsustainable use

Only around 20 per cent of unwanted electronics (e-waste) are recycled globally. That means that all the energy and resources that went into producing them, as well as the rare-earth metals which are so toxic to extract, are simply going to waste.

In 2016, 44.7 million metric tonnes of e-waste were created, equivalent to

4,500
EIFFEL TOWERS.

Not so green

Even when electronics do get 'recycled', this is often not done in an eco-friendly way. At 'recycling plants' in countries such as China and Ghana, poorly paid workers, including children, break electronic goods open to get to the valuable components inside. This is done using dangerous chemicals or by burning the objects, which gives off toxic fumes. The rest of the object, such as the plastic shell, then gets thrown away.

A pile of plastic monitor shells in Ghana

Designed to fail

One of the biggest factors that drives so much electronic waste is the way the items are designed in the first place. Batteries in smartphones stop working properly after a couple of years, and their screens and buttons are easily broken. Yet it often costs more to try to fix a damaged item than buy a new one. Many models are made so that broken parts can't be replaced, and tech companies stop releasing software upgrades for old models. This means consumers have no choice but to buy a whole new device, and the old one is thrown out.

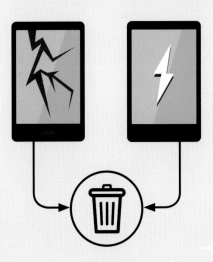

BEYOND RECYCLING

We are all familiar with the idea of recycling: objects get sent away to be turned into totally new things. But breaking an object down into separate materials, and then reforming those materials into something new still uses energy and other resources. There is a lot more we can do with our stuff before we recycle it in the standard way.

Reusing

When it comes to reducing the environmental impact of our stuff, the first thing we can do is use things for longer. Instead of getting a new phone every year, keep using the model you have. Or, give it to a friend or resell it to a second-hand distributor so that someone else can use it in its existing form. Product designers can help with this step by creating devices to be as long-lasting and durable as possible.

It's better to use devices for longer than to keep buying new ones.

Refurbishing

The second way that product designers and manufacturers can help make products more environmentally friendly is by making them so that they can be easily repaired or upgraded. For example, smartphones could be designed so the screen, battery or hardware can be changed or upgraded without having to replace the entire phone.

A technician replacing the battery in a smartphone

Remanufacturing

After refurbishment comes remanufacturing. This process involves sending items back to a factory where they can be broken down into parts, then rebuilt with a mixture of old and new components. This way, any bits of an item that are still perfectly usable get a second life in a new object, rather than being thrown away with the broken parts.

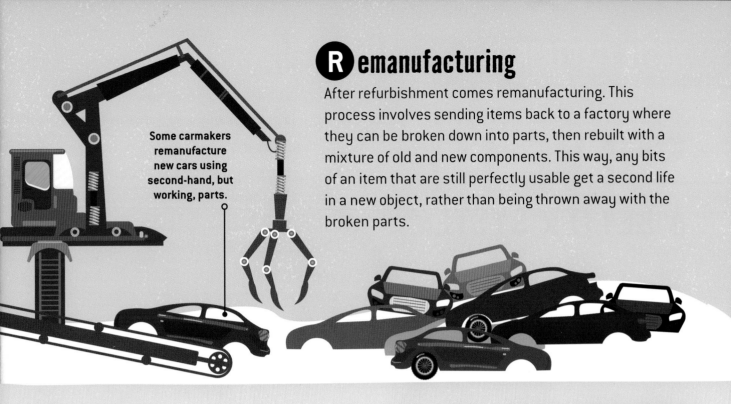

Some carmakers remanufacture new cars using second-hand, but working, parts.

Recycling

The final process is recycling, where an object is broken down back into pure materials such as plastic, glass or metal. These materials can then be reformed into totally new items. Allowing for 100 per cent recycling of an item requires designing it in such a way that all the materials can be easily separated at the end of the item's use.

Metal that has been sorted for recycling.

SPOTLIGHT:
CIRCULAR ECONOMY

Remember the linear system on page 6? An alternative to that is known as the 'circular economy'. Instead of extracting materials, using them briefly, then throwing them away, in a circular economy materials are used for as long as possible, then reused for something else. Nothing is ever wasted, and fewer raw materials are needed.

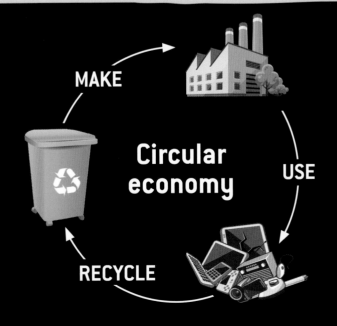

MAKE

Circular economy

USE

RECYCLE

SOLVE IT!
A BETTER SYSTEM

A circular system of reusing, refurbishing, remanufacturing and recycling is far more eco-friendly than our current linear system. Look at the diagram of a circular system for mobile phones below. Can you match the labels to the images? There are labels for places, and labels for actions.

1 Consumer (user of phone)

2 Shop (sales and repairs)

3 Factory (manufacture and remanufacture)

4 Recycling centre (materials recycling)

5 REUSE

6 REFURBISH

7 REMANUFACTURE

8 RECYCLE

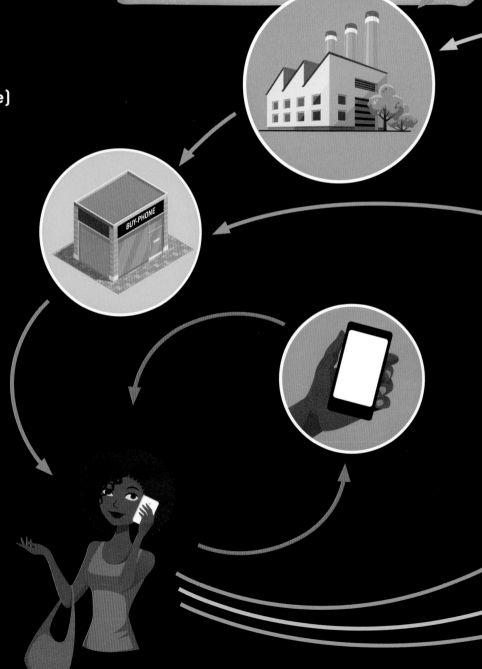

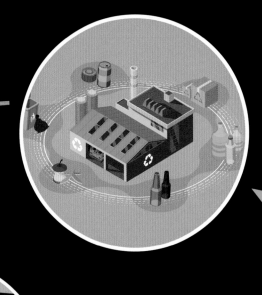

CAN YOU SOLVE IT?

Look at the images in the diagram and then look at the labels of places and actions. Can you figure out:

Which matches with which?

▶ Why some of the loops are smaller than others?

In a muddle?
Turn to page 45
for the answer.

TEST IT!
MAKE A CIRCUIT GAME

If you have spare power cord from an old broken appliance such as a kettle, lamp or iron, don't chuck it out – remanufacture it into this circuit game.

YOU WILL NEED

the power cord from a broken appliance or extension cord at least 50 cm long with the plug cut off (ask an adult to do this)

wire strippers or pliers

a small buzzer
(available from electrical stores)

a 9v battery

electrical tape

a piece of cardboard 40 cm x 10 cm

a pencil

STEP ①

Ask an adult to strip the rubber coating off the outside of the cord. To do this with pliers, apply moderate pressure to the cord with the cutting blades, and twist the cord around to cut through the rubber, leaving the wires inside intact. Once cut, pull the piece of rubber coating off. It's easiest to strip the cord a couple of centimetres at a time.

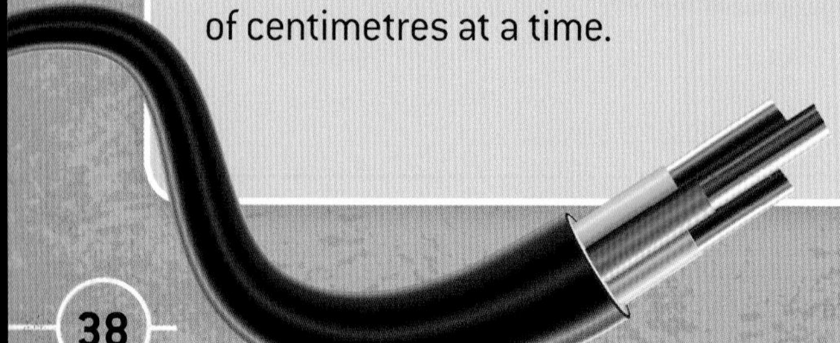

STEP ②

Inside the cord you should find two or three smaller insulated copper wires. Cut two pieces of insulated wire 50 cm long. Ask an adult to strip some of the rubber coating from these, too. On the first piece, strip 6 cm off one end, and 2 cm off the other (the green wire on the picture opposite). On the second piece, strip all the coating off except for 10 cm at one end (the blue wire opposite).

STEP ③

Bend your cardboard
into a frame, by folding
10 cm at either end vertically.
Poke a hole in the vertical piece at either
end using the pencil.

STEP ④

Take your first wire, and loop
the stripped 6 cm part round
and twist it into a closed circle.
Thread your second piece of
wire through the loop.

STEP ⑤

Poke the insulated end of the second wire
through the left-hand hole in the frame
so that 2 cm of insulation is on the inside,
and the rest is outside. Bend the long
stripped part into a zigzag, and poke the
other end out through the right-hand hole.

STEP ⑥

Tape the stripped end of the zigzag
wire to the negative terminal on
the 9v battery. Tape the red wire on
the buzzer to the positive terminal
on the battery. Finally, connect
the black wire from the buzzer to
the end of the first loop wire by
twisting, then taping them together.
This completes the circuit.

STEP ⑦

Your game is ready to play. See if
you can move the wire loop around
the wire zigzag without sounding
the buzzer.

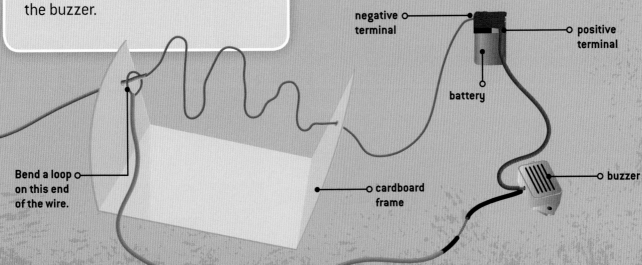

negative
terminal

positive
terminal

battery

Bend a loop
on this end
of the wire.

cardboard
frame

buzzer

THE FUTURE OF STUFF

Many businesses and individuals are aware of the problems of overconsumption, and are changing their practices and behaviours so as to have less impact on the environment. Here are some ways people are already doing things differently:

Minimalism

Various studies have shown that once people's basic needs are met, buying more and more stuff doesn't make them happier. There's always something new and shiny to want, and it becomes an endless cycle. Some people are rejecting the 'more more more' cycle by becoming 'minimalist' – living with a small number of possessions and focusing on the things in life that they feel are most important.

Friends enjoying the sunshine and each other's company – all for free!

Forget owning

In the future we might think quite differently about what is 'ours'. Instead of buying things like fridges or furniture outright and then having to dispose of them ourselves, we could pay a subscription for them, similar to the subscriptions we have for music and films already. When we want to upgrade or replace a broken item we would simply return it to the shop, who would supply a new model and remanufacture the working parts of the old one.

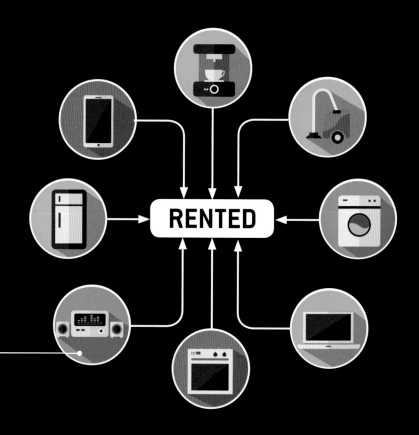

All sorts of items including home appliances might be rented instead of bought.

Circular systems

In a perfect circular economy, waste would not exist. Everything that is currently considered waste could be used in making something else. Different businesses could be connected in loops, for example waste fish poo from a fish farm could be used to fertilise the soil on a fruit and veg farm. Food waste from the fruit and veg produced by a food processing plant (such as vegetable peelings or fruit cores) could be fed to the fish, creating a loop (see below).

Smart objects

Tablets and smartphones aren't all bad, if we aren't replacing them all the time. One big environmental benefit is that these are multifunctional devices. A smartphone for example can replace physical books, maps, notepads, a calculator, a music player, a radio, a telephone, a camera and more. In the future our technology might combine even more functions, reducing the use of materials, water and energy.

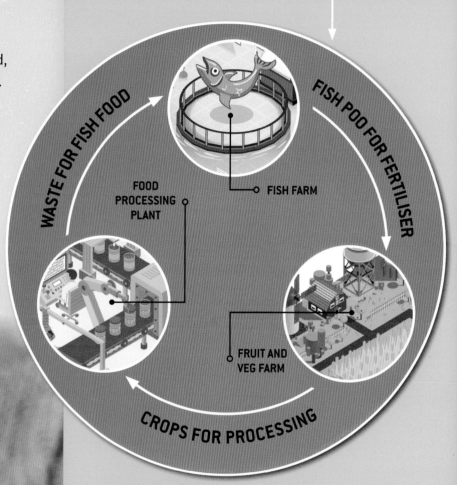

FISH FARM

WASTE FOR FISH FOOD

FISH POO FOR FERTILISER

FOOD PROCESSING PLANT

FRUIT AND VEG FARM

CROPS FOR PROCESSING

SPOTLIGHT: BIOMIMETICS

A biomimetic approach to design means copying the way nature does things. In nature, nothing is wasted, because all waste is food for something else. A circular system of making things mimics the way nature recycles everything.

ANSWERS

Did you figure out what each of the examples had in common? The answer is that they are all ways of getting or enjoying 'new' things without new physical objects being made. The examples cover several different ways to avoid extra things being produced, including:

DIGITAL OR VIRTUAL GOODS

Streaming films or music online doesn't require physical items such as CDs or DVDs to be made from raw materials, shipped and sold to consumers. However, there are still impacts on the environment if people are replacing their electronic devices regularly.

HIRING NOT BUYING

In the examples of the bicycle hire scheme or the clothing subscription, many people can make use of the same items. This reduces the number of individual items that need to be produced. If 15 different people all use the same hire bike in one day instead of buying their own, far fewer bicycles need to be made.

SWAPPING AND GIFTING

'Swishing' goods with your friends or posting them online to share with your local community is another way of helping people get things for free that are new to them, without items being made from scratch.

sharing economy

As buyers and wearers of clothes, we have the power to support sustainable clothing manufacturers, and can ensure that our clothing is used and disposed of responsibly. The more people making informed choices about their shopping, the greater the benefit to the environment will be.

Here's one example of the sort of poster you could create:

HOW TO BUY CLOTHES SUSTAINABLY

CHOOSE ▶ clothes made from eco-friendly fibres such as organic cotton or hemp, NOT plastic polyester

USE ▶ your clothes for as long as possible; repair tears or missing buttons instead of throwing them out

LOSE ▶ unwanted garments to the charity shop or textile recycling where they can be used by someone else, made into new clothes or composted

You might prefer to illustrate your poster, or add in more facts and figures. Whatever you create, put it up somewhere lots of people will be able to see it.

SOLVE IT! ECO-FRIENDLY PAPER PAGES 28–29

As with clothing, environmental improvements to paper manufacturing can be made at each stage, from the harvesting of raw materials through manufacture, use and disposal. Here is a flowchart showing how paper can be made and used in a more eco-friendly way.

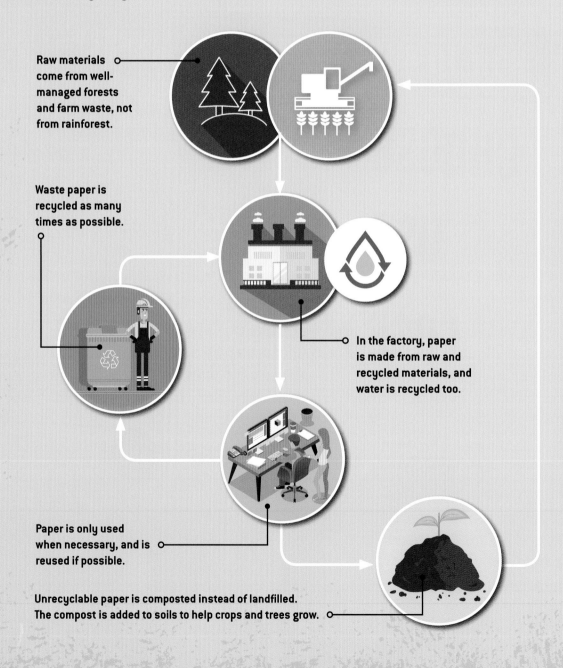

Raw materials come from well-managed forests and farm waste, not from rainforest.

Waste paper is recycled as many times as possible.

In the factory, paper is made from raw and recycled materials, and water is recycled too.

Paper is only used when necessary, and is reused if possible.

Unrecyclable paper is composted instead of landfilled. The compost is added to soils to help crops and trees grow.

In this circular system, the tighter loops in the centre of the circle use the least amount of energy. For example, reusing an old mobile phone or buying one second-hand requires little or no energy. Refurbishing and remanufacturing use a little more, and recycling materials uses the most, so this loop is the biggest. But importantly, nothing is wasted at any stage.

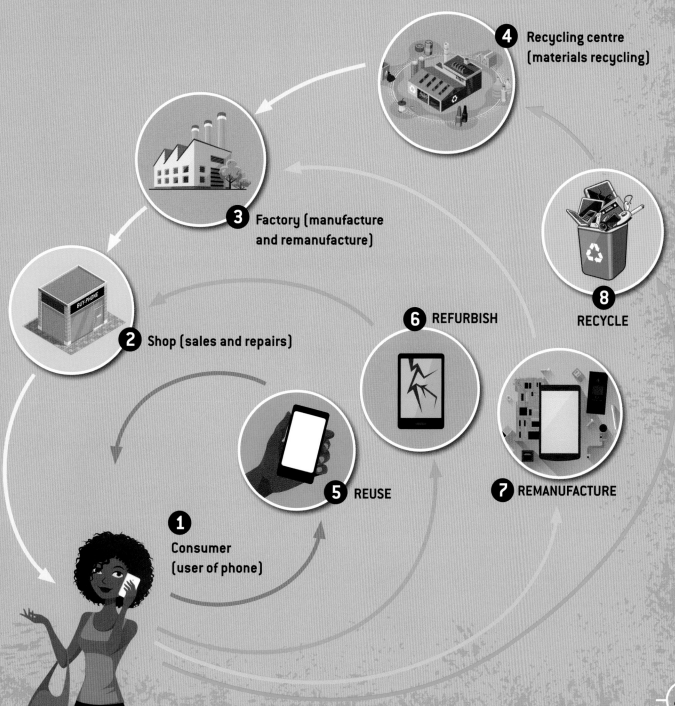

4 Recycling centre (materials recycling)

3 Factory (manufacture and remanufacture)

2 Shop (sales and repairs)

6 REFURBISH

8 RECYCLE

5 REUSE

7 REMANUFACTURE

1 Consumer (user of phone)

WHAT YOU CAN DO

The activities in this book should already have given you some ideas about how you can help to reduce consumption, but here are a few other tips for how to make a difference.

Buy second-hand

Do your shopping in charity shops or on online sites such as eBay. Charity shops have the double benefit of reducing impacts on the environment, as well as supporting good causes. You can donate your old stuff to charity shops when it doesn't fit anymore, too.

Buy quality

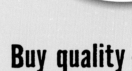

If you do need to buy new things, and it isn't something you'll grow out of, then make sure you buy stuff that is good quality and will last. Having to constantly replace cheap, mass-produced items is not only bad for the environment, but it's also more expensive in the long run.

MAKE, DON'T BUY

Instead of going clothes shopping as a fun activity, try making things yourself. Learning to sew is a very rewarding skill as it allows you to make totally unique outfits, as well giving you the ability to fix your favourite garments when they get torn or damaged.

GLOSSARY

assembly line a line of workers and machines that an item moves along as it is being put together in a factory

biodegrade to break down naturally in the environment

biomimetic describes a human-made object or a process that copies the way nature does things

circular economy a way of making things where materials are reused again and again, rather than being used once and thrown away

climate change the changes in world weather patterns caused by human activity

consumerism the idea that it's good to keep buying new things

consumption the act of using up a resource, or buying new things

crude oil oil that was formed underground over millions of years, and is used to make fuels, chemicals and plastics

deforestation the act of cutting down forests

e-waste electronic items that are thrown away

ecological footprint the amount of natural resources (such as land, water and air) that it takes to support a person

ecosystem all of the living things such as plants and animals, and the non-living things such as rocks, in a particular area

emissions something that has been released or put out into the world, such as gases from a factory

extraction the act of taking a resource out of the ground or the natural landscape

fast fashion clothing designs that move quickly from the runway to the shops, are bought by people and then thrown away after a short time

fossil fuel a fuel such as oil or coal that was formed over millions of years from dead plants and animals

greenhouse gas a gas in the Earth's atmosphere that traps heat from the Sun, gradually causing the Earth to warm up

irrigation watering crops

landfill a large hole in the ground where rubbish is dumped

mass production a method of quickly making large quantities of a particular object

methane a powerful greenhouse gas

microfibre a very small piece of artificial fibre

minimalism a lifestyle that avoids buying and owning a lot of objects, and values non-material things instead

organic plants that are grown without the use of artificial chemicals

pesticide a chemical used to kill off unwanted insects

radioactive something that gives off damaging rays

raw material the basic, original material from which something is made

recycle to break an item down and reform it into a new object

refurbish to fix or upgrade an item

remanufacture to use the parts from an old object in making a new object

renewable used to describe something that doesn't run out or get used up

subscription an amount of money paid regularly in order to receive an item or a service

sustainable describes any practice that can be carried out continuously without using up natural resources or causing harm to the environment

swishing an activity where people get together to swap old clothes

upcycle to make an object into something new, without breaking down the original object

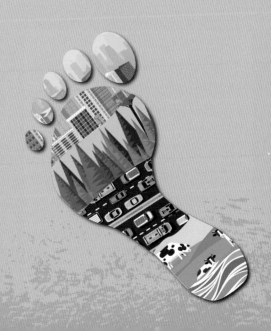